AIR FORCE SPECIAL OPERATIONS COMMAND

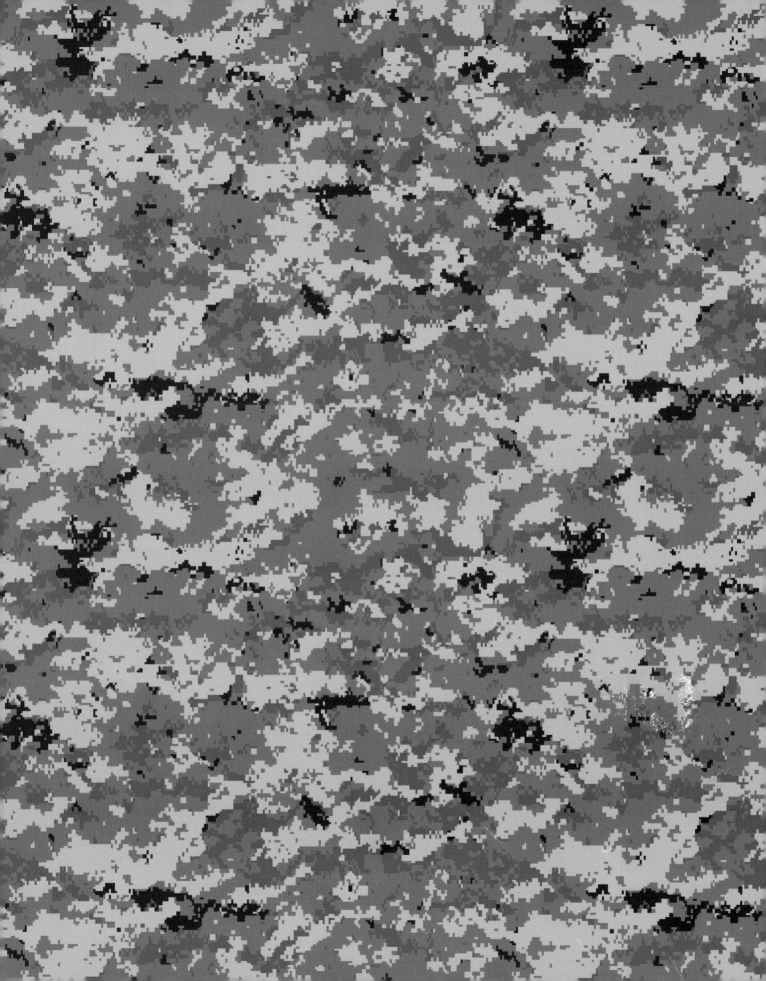

U.S. SPECIAL FORCES

# AIR FORCE SPECIAL OPERATIONS COMMAND

JIM WHITING

CREATIVE ✿ EDUCATION

**PUBLISHED BY** Creative Education

P.O. Box 227, Mankato, Minnesota 56002

*Creative Education is an imprint of The Creative Company*

www.thecreativecompany.us

**DESIGN AND PRODUCTION BY** Christine Vanderbeek

**ART DIRECTION BY** Rita Marshall

**PRINTED IN** the United States of America

**PHOTOGRAPHS BY**

Alamy (Everett Collection Historical, Lightroom Photos, PF-[MIL],
PF-[mil2], Planetpix, US Air Force Photo), Corbis (AP, Ed Darack/
Science Faction, DOD, David Howells, Reuters, Jim Sugar, US Air Force
– digital version c/Science Faction), Department of Defense (Glenn
Fawcett), iStockphoto (spxChrome), Shutterstock (ALMAGAMI, gst),
SuperStock (Photri Inc./age fotostock, Dan Sheehan/Science Faction,
StockTrek/Purestock, Stocktrek Images, US Air Force Photo/Staff Sgt
Jonathan Snyder)

**LIBRARY OF CONGRESS CATALOGING-IN-PUBLICATION DATA**

Whiting, Jim.

Air Force Special Operations Command / Jim Whiting.

p. cm. — (U.S. Special Forces)

Includes bibliographical references and index.

*Summary: A chronological account of the American special forces*
*unit known as Air Force Special Ops, including key details about*
*important figures, landmark missions, and controversies.*

**ISBN 978-1-60818-460-6**

1. United States. Air Force—Commando troops—Juvenile literature.
2. United States. Air Force Special Operations Command—Juvenile
literature. 3. Special forces (Military science)—United States—
Juvenile literature. 4. Special operations (Military science)—Juvenile
literature. I. Title.

UG633.W44 2014

358.4—dc23   2013036169

**CCSS:** RI.5.1, 2, 3, 8; RH.6-8.4, 5, 6, 8

**FIRST EDITION**

9 8 7 6 5 4 3 2 1

**U.S. SPECIAL FORCES**

# TABLE OF CONTENTS

★ ★ ★

The airframe, or body, of Hercules planes can be converted for multiple uses, such as a gunship.

**U.S. SPECIAL FORCES**

# INTRODUCTION

As United States Commander-in-Chief General Norman Schwarzkopf began making plans to liberate Kuwait after Iraqi dictator Saddam Hussein's invasion in August 1990, his first objective was to knock out two radar installations near the Iraqi border. Those "electronic eyes" provided a significant obstacle to American aircraft that would attack Hussein. Eliminating them would make it much safer for those aircraft to conduct their missions. Schwarzkopf asked Colonel George Gray of the Air Force Special Operations Command (AFSOC) if he could guarantee that the mission—code-named "Plan Eager Anvil"—would be completely successful.

"Yes, sir," Gray responded.

"You get to start the war," Schwarzkopf said.

Plan Eager Anvil started shortly after midnight on January 17, 1991. Four AFSOC Pave Low helicopters equipped with a variety of electronic aids led eight heavily armed U.S. Army Apache attack helicopters. The AFSOC pilots realized that the stakes were high. "Oh, my gosh, the weight of the world is on this mission," said one. "A lot of people could die if we fail."

Skimming over several hundred miles of terrain at a maximum elevation of 50 feet (15 m), the pilots zigzagged back and forth to avoid radar detection. Their navigation was flawless. At 2:38 A.M. they arrived at the target. The Apaches began their barrage, raining down missiles, rockets, and machine gunfire on the radar stations. Four minutes later, both facilities were obliterated. Soon afterward, a massive air armada headed for Iraq. There was no interference. AFSOC had done its job.

*General Schwarzkopf retired in 1992 after serving an illustrious career in the military.*

# LITTLE-KNOWN YET MUCH-APPRECIATED

**U.S. SPECIAL FORCES**

VERY FEW PEOPLE OUTSIDE THE U.S. MILITARY COMMUNITY are aware of AFSOC's existence. Perhaps that is because AFSOC's primary responsibility is to lead and transport other units to the point of attack and then support them, rather than perform the headline-grabbing operation. As writer Bob Drury noted in *Men's Health* magazine, "Let us face reality: the Navy SEALs get all the ink, the Army Rangers all the glory, the Marine Recons all the babes. Conversely, to the average guy on the street the mention of U.S. Air Force Special Operators inevitably elicits a look of bewilderment. *The Air Force has those guys?*"

"Those guys" have roots reaching back to World War II (1939–45). Flying modified B-24 Liberator bombers painted black, aircrews called Carpetbaggers became proficient in low-level missions that were often conducted in bad weather through a variety of European terrain. Those missions usually involved dropping supplies to groups resisting German occupation, distributing *propaganda* leaflets, and depositing agents of the Office of Strategic Services (OSS, the forerunner of the modern Central Intelligence Agency, or CIA). Similar aircrews, known as No. 1 Air Commando Group, played key roles in the China-Burma-India *Theater of Operations*. Flying aircraft such as the C-47 Dakota Transport and twin-engine B-25 Mitchell bombers, the men flew over mountains and jungles to supply British commandos operating deep behind Japanese lines. Pleased with the unit's courage and competence, a British officer wrote, "Please be assured that we will go with your boys Any Place, Any Time, Any Where." From those

*The B-25 was named for General Billy Mitchell, known as the "Father of the U.S. Air Force."*

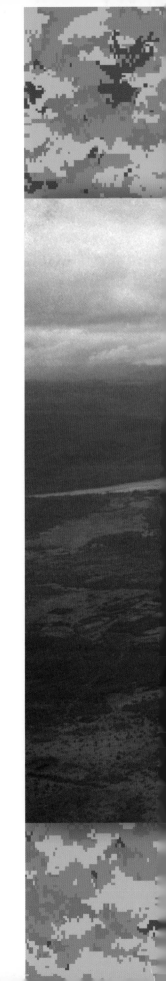

**FORCE FACTS** Only one C-130 special operations aircraft has been lost in a combat mission over enemy territory, and that happened in 1967 at the height of the Vietnam War.

comments came AFSOC's motto: "Anytime, Anywhere."

When the war ended, so did the air commandos' services. Then, as American forces became increasingly involved in the Vietnam War during the 1960s and early 1970s, the air force's World War II-era skills were dusted off and updated with more weaponry. Some C-47s were fitted with three 7.6-millimeter, 6-barrel mini-guns mounted on the left side. Nicknamed "Puff the Magic Dragon," these aircraft provided close air support at night for troops on the ground. As a C-47 pilot circled the target area, he used a sighting system over his left shoulder to pump out 6,000 rounds a minute from the 3 guns. "Whoever built 'Puff' had a sick mind," said an anonymous soldier who witnessed—and benefited from—its firepower. "At night it looked like a red line of light coming from the heavens, like Hell leaking fire."

An even more lethal "bird" during this era was the AC-130 Spectre, a modified C-130 Hercules transport aircraft bristling with weaponry. Its chief armament was a 105-millimeter cannon that fired 42-pound (19 kg), 31-inch-long (79 cm) projectiles. A single round could take out a tank, and several successive shots could topple a building. A 40-millimeter cannon destroyed trucks and lightly armored vehicles. Finally, a pair of 20-millimeter Vulcan cannons firing 40 rounds per second could kill enemy soldiers. Vietnam also marked the wartime debut of two *iconic* helicopters: the CH-47 Chinook and the HH-53 "Jolly Green Giant." Both would play key roles in special operations during future conflicts.

At the peak of American involvement in Vietnam, more than 10,000 U.S. Air Force special forces personnel and 500 aircraft were involved. The 1970 raid on the Son Tay prisoner of war (POW) camp, located in North Vietnam, was one of the group's most notable missions. Helicopter pilots—contributing to a total of nearly 30 aircraft and 100 airmen involved in the operation—transported Army Special Forces personnel to the camp. Unbeknownst to mission planners, the prisoners had been moved elsewhere shortly

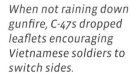

*When not raining down gunfire, C-47s dropped leaflets encouraging Vietnamese soldiers to switch sides.*

**FORCE FACTS** The first combat parachute operation involving members of two American armed forces occurred in Vietnam in 1967. Eight combat controllers jumped with elements of the army's 173rd Airborne Brigade.

before the raid. Yet the operation itself proceeded almost flawlessly and provided a huge boost in morale among POWs. However, when the war ended in 1975, virtually all special forces—including the air force's—again fell into disuse. Special forces spending dropped to 0.1 percent of total federal defense spending.

World events soon brought special forces back to the forefront. A wave of terrorism that began with the murder of 11 members of the Israeli team at the 1972 Summer Olympics in Munich, West Germany, culminated 7 years later. In defiance of international law, Iranian militants overran the American embassy in Tehran and seized dozens of hostages. The U.S. devised a plan called Operation Eagle Claw to rescue them. Launched in April 1980, the operation ended in disaster. Eight servicemen were killed, and the would-be rescuers never got close to their objective. The failure stained the reputation of U.S. special forces internationally but spawned the formation of the U.S. Special Operations Command (SOCOM) in 1987. The new command structure brought all U.S. special forces together so that operations could be better coordinated in the future.

*Guns of all sizes were put to use as forces went out on rescue missions in Vietnam.*

AFSOC—the air force's component of SOCOM—was born on May 22, 1990, with its headquarters at Florida's Hurlburt Field. It integrated a number of different units into a single command.

As special forces expert Fred Pushies notes, the mission of AFSOC is "to provide mobility, surgical firepower, *covert* tanker support, and special tactics teams." The first three tasks involve employing aircrews of both fixed-wing aircraft and helicopters to fly under hazardous conditions. AFSOC's special tactics teams (STTs) perform several vital functions for success in modern warfare: they provide combat air control, prepare landing zones for conventional forces, recover downed pilots, treat battlefield

injuries, give detailed weather information of target areas, and more. Usually, AFSOC operates alongside other American special forces. It may also work directly with foreign governments and their respective military organizations.

A few months after AFSOC's formation, Hussein's invasion of Kuwait provided the opportunity for AFSOC to put its skills to the test. Plan Eager Anvil was just the beginning. AFSOC successfully performed a variety of other missions that played crucial roles in driving the Iraqi invaders out of Kuwait. The same was true a decade later, when terrorists attacked the World Trade Center in New York and the Pentagon in Washington, D.C., on September 11, 2001. The event catapulted the U.S. into what has become known as the War on Terror. Acting on intelligence that Afghanistan—at that time controlled by the *Taliban*—had provided a safe haven and training sites for the attackers, the U.S. responded by sending special forces to the country. AFSOC not only provided transport to Afghanistan, but once there, it also contributed skilled fighters.

AFSOC underwent a significant geographical expansion in 2006, when several elements of the outfit made their way west to

*The Munich Massacre ended at a German airport, with hostages and terrorists dying in gunfire and explosions.*

New Mexico's Cannon Air Force Base. The move presented several advantages. One was that the dispersal of forces prevented the entire operation from being shut down in the event of adverse weather situations, such as hurricanes, which had previously closed Hurlburt for days at a time. Another benefit to being in New Mexico was having clear flying weather for at least 300 days each year. A third was the access to Melrose Training Range, a sprawling expanse of empty land that not only provided a live-fire range for gunships but also a variety of terrain in which assault teams could practice. Several short dirt airstrips mimic those that operators are likely to encounter in other parts of the world. And the elevation of the base—which in some areas approaches a mile (1.6 km) above sea level—approximates that of many global hot spots where AFSOC is likely to go, eliminating the need for an operator to adjust to reduced oxygen at those levels.

★ ★ ★

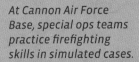

*At Cannon Air Force Base, special ops teams practice firefighting skills in simulated cases.*

**FORCE FACTS** Pararescue training often includes riding with Emergency Medical Service (EMS) personnel in high-crime areas of large cities to gain experience in treating gunshot wounds.

# TRAINING TO BE THE TOP

AT A TIME WHEN TRADITIONAL AMERICAN MILITARY FORCES are being downsized because of federal budget reductions, special forces are on the upswing. Budgets for both army and navy special forces have increased by more than 25 percent since 2006. Correspondingly, demands on AFSOC to get these men to and from their targets—and support them while they are there—have also intensified. Another area of rapid growth affecting AFSOC is aviation foreign internal defense (FID). At the time of 9/11, the 6th Special Operations Squadron—the AFSOC unit tasked with FID—had just 85 personnel. By 2015, that number will increase to at least 700.

In years past, the majority of pilots and aircrew members tended to complete at least one other tour of duty before joining AFSOC. Now, about two-thirds of newly minted airmen go directly to AFSOC. Since the year 2000, the number of airmen who undergo the 6-month-long AFSOC training course has quadrupled, from fewer than 1,000 to more than 4,000. An increasing number of these personnel are women, who fill every role from pilot to *loadmaster*. In 2009, Lieutenant Colonel Brenda Cartier became the first female to command an AFSOC flying squadron when she took control of the 4th Special Operations Squadron Ghostriders Hercules gunships.

Some training for this influx of personnel involves interactive computer gaming. For example, airmen can click on virtual switches to learn their functions, rather than spending time on

*The role of a pararescue specialist was not one open to women recruits as of 2013.*

> **FORCE FACTS** Pararescuemen wear maroon berets to symbolize their devotion to duty and selflessness in living up to their motto "That others may live."

the flight line in actual cockpits—which ties down the aircraft and makes them unavailable for missions—with instructors watching them. Eventually, AFSOC plans on making these applications available on mobile devices such as iPods and iPads.

There is also an emphasis on training with a flight simulator in combination with stationary crew station trainers. In a simulated scenario, pilots and engineers "fly" the aircraft, while other crew members—such as navigators (who continually monitor the aircraft's position) and fire control officers (who are responsible for overseeing aircraft weaponry)—carry out their assigned tasks and stay in constant radio contact with each other. In some cases, the simulators can be linked to live aircraft for maximum realism.

Given the increasing numbers and complexity of real-world missions, most graduates are *deployed* within a few weeks with little opportunity to "ease into" combat situations. Defense writer Grace Jean describes a typical operation, involving a gunship aiding a special forces patrol that has been ambushed. "The gunship crew is told that they are cleared to fire on the enemy in close proximity to the friendly forces who are struggling to pull their casualties to safety," she writes. "The *infrared* sensor operator, who was on his first deployment, keeps his crosshairs firmly on the enemy targets. The radio calls between the navigator and crew proceed calmly as the rounds take out the enemy." The operator isn't the only one feeling the pressure. Gunners must be able to place their rounds accurately within "danger close" ranges, which can be less than 137 yards (125 m) from friendly forces.

The number of ground-based STT personnel has also undergone a significant increase. Unlike some other U.S. special forces, in which candidates must be currently serving in the military, STT candidates can enlist in the air force and begin training for one of three specialties: combat control, pararescue, and special operations weather.

Combat controllers (CCTs) are certified Federal Aviation

*Simulated training environments aim to replicate actual circumstances as closely as possible.*

**FORCE FACTS** Part of scuba training involves using a re-breather, which doesn't allow air bubbles to rise to the surface of the water and give away the presence of the operator.

Administration (FAA) air traffic controllers who provide the link between aircraft and special operations forces on the ground. They establish assault zones, conduct air traffic control, and direct fire support.

Pararescuemen (also known as "PJs," for parajumpers) have a pedigree as long as their pilot brethren, tracing their origins back to the same China-Burma-India Theater of Operations in World War II. Since then, they have been in constant demand, even working with American space programs. They are the only U.S. military personnel specifically trained in personnel recovery and rescue in combat situations. Because a high percentage of those they rescue are wounded—sometimes badly—they receive extensive training in treating battlefield trauma.

Special operations weathermen are meteorologists who gather weather and other environmental data in hostile territory for use in the planning and execution of special operations missions. This information is especially vital in countries such as Afghanistan, where weather conditions can change significantly within minutes. As the 5th-century B.C. Chinese general and military strategist Sun Tzu wrote, "Know the ground, know the weather; your victory will then be total."

As of 2013, all STT personnel were men. Anyone interested in joining STT must be willing to make a commitment to training that may last for up to two years or even longer to ensure that a potential team member will be fully prepared to confront combat situations. As journalist Bob Drury explains, STTs "must be able to climb mountains, *rappel* from helicopters, dive beneath rivers and oceans, survive in arid deserts, free-fall from airplanes at recklessly high altitudes, and be proficient in all manner of communications and weaponry ... with a catch. Each must

*Teamwork enables weathermen to remain safe while determining wind speed and other conditions.*

perform all of these tasks as well as every man in the SEAL, Ranger, or Marine units to which they are attached."

And that's just for starters. As a longtime combat controller observes, "It's hard to be the guy that kicks the door in *and* the guy who controls the aircraft *and* the guy who coordinates the communications between the two." In other words, STTs have to be as proficient in combat situations as other special forces—while also performing the duties of their specialty flawlessly.

STT's creator, Colonel John T. Carney, adds, "We provided the communications [special forces] needed to get to the target, to lay close support or gunship fire on the target, to bring in the aircraft or helicopters that would haul them out of trouble. And we had to do it with whatever we could carry on our backs."

Because an extraordinary degree of physical fitness is essential for the job, every candidate must pass the Physical Ability Stamina Test (PAST). It consists of six individual tests, each of which has a standard minimum time or number of repetitions: two 25-meter underwater swims without coming up for air, with 3 minutes rest between each leg; a 500-meter swim; a 1.5-mile (2.4

*In addition to basic training, pararescuemen hone survival skills in various environments.*

km) run; plus pull-ups, sit-ups, and pushups. Then the candidate spends at least two weeks in selection training for his respective specialty, testing his motivation and willingness to completely commit to long-term training.

Training is grueling. Part of the process involves learning how to arrive at targeted destinations via such methods as parachuting, scuba diving, rappelling and *fast-roping*, riding in small rubber boats, and driving all-terrain vehicles. Mastering these different methods takes up a considerable amount of training time. Trainees also learn small-group tactics for future use in cooperating with and teaching other military forces. At some point, everyone goes to Fairchild Air Force Base near Spokane, Washington for Survival, Evasion, Resistance, and Escape (SERE) training. This course instructs the men in how to avoid capture or how to act if they are taken prisoner. And, of course, STT trainees spend considerable amounts of time learning how to shoot.

Special forces trainers ratchet up the intensity of training by increasing the stress levels associated with seemingly routine tasks. During the water phase of training, for example, trainees "buddy breathe" by taking turns using a single snorkel. As writer Scott Gourley notes, "The STT twist is to simulate the physical and mental challenges of a real combat situation. A mountainous Air Force instructor adds this extra note of realism by joining the trainees in the pool, where he proceeds to climb on their backs, yank off their masks, hold their heads underwater, and try to block their airways." The end product, as former AFSOC Chief Master Sergeant Bob Martens points out, is that these "ordinary people ... are doing extraordinary things, day in and day out."

Even when STTs are not deployed, training doesn't let up. The men commonly put in 8- to 10-hour days in the gym, on the running track, in the pool, and in the classroom to continually hone their skills and keep pace with the latest developments in their field.

*Members of the 720th Special Tactics Group train to be able to rescue fellow personnel from the water.*

**FORCE FACTS** Parachute training includes both HAHO (high altitude, high opening) and HALO (high altitude, low opening) scenarios. The trainees jump from the aircraft at altitudes of between 15,000 and 35,000 feet (4,600–11,000 m).

# GEAR FOR GETTING THE JOB DONE

U.S. SPECIAL FORCES

BECAUSE OF THE NATURE OF ITS ASSIGNMENTS, AFSOC utilizes an especially wide array of equipment, from aircraft to gear on the ground. The workhorse of AFSOC aircraft is the four-engine C-130 Hercules. It has remained in service ever since its maiden flight in 1955, aided by improvements and adaptations befitting conditions of contemporary warfare. Nearly 100 feet (30 m) long and with a wingspan greater than 130 feet (40 m), the Hercules can be used in several ways. As a gunship, it provides devastating firepower in close air support (CAS). With a range of more than 2,200 miles (3,540 km) and inflight refueling capacity, gunships can stay on station for hours on end. Even if they aren't actively engaged in CAS, gunships provide an important psychological lift. As Lieutenant Colonel Tim Schaffer notes, "It gave the troops on the ground peace of mind to hear the drone of those engines overhead, just in case."

In recent years, a 25-millimeter Gatling gun has replaced the original 20-millimeter weapon in the gunships. It can fire up to 1,800 rounds a minute from altitudes of nearly 2.5 miles (4 km). The spent brass *casings* are automatically ejected into a holding container inside the aircraft, thus avoiding the hazards of airmen slipping during a mission and the time-consuming labor of shoveling them out of the fuselage when the aircraft returns to base. These weapons systems—as well as advanced electronics

*Originally designed to carry troops and cargo, the C-130 has grown increasingly versatile over the years.*

that enable the Hercules to fly in almost any weather conditions—are so intricate that the latest version of the C-130—the AC-130U "Spooky"—has a more complex wiring system than a space shuttle. Future variations are likely to be even more complicated as the capability of firing rockets and missiles is added to the gunships' already formidable armament.

A second C-130 mission is providing long-range delivery of special operations forces to their targets. Known as the Combat Talon II, this version boasts advanced electronics and is capable of insertions either by airdrop or by landing in very compact areas. It can fly as low as 250 feet (75 m) to minimize its chances of detection. The Combat Shadow, which provides mid-air refueling for helicopters and fixed-wing aircraft, is a third variant of the C-130. The Rivet Rider Commando Solo is tasked with psychological operations against enemies—to undermine their morale—and broadcasting, as well as with electronic countermeasures. It served as the "Voice of the Gulf" during Operation Desert Storm in 1991, broadcasting surrender terms to disheartened Iraqi soldiers. The aircraft also dropped 17 million leaflets into Iraqi positions, leaving them with the chilling message that "This could have been a real bomb."

For years, the other primary AFSOC aircraft was the MH-53 Pave Low helicopter, which at 90 feet (27 m) in length was nearly as long as the Hercules. The Pave Low also boasted a long and distinguished pedigree, dating back to the Vietnam War and the Jolly Green Giant helicopter, and operating long beyond its expected lifetime. It has been replaced by the Bell-Boeing CV-22 Osprey tilt-rotor vertical lift aircraft, which takes off like a helicopter and then flies like a fixed-wing airplane by rotating its two *nacelles* into a forward-facing position. The craft is packed with electronics that enable it to function effectively at low altitude in foul weather and hostile environments. While, at 57 feet (17.4 m), it is considerably shorter than its predecessor—carrying 24

*In 2008, the remaining Pave Lows still in active service (of the 72 produced) were retired.*

Special operations weathermen wear pewter berets, with a crest that includes four bolts of lightning, a combat knife, and a parachute.

fully equipped troops as opposed to 38 in Pave Lows—it has more than twice the range and double the speed, allowing it to carry out operations in a single period of darkness. Former AFSOC commander Lieutenant General Michael Woolsey once said, "I think [the Osprey] is going to truly transform the way we do business by giving us rapid mobility on the battlefield for our special operators that we have not had before."

A third aircraft integral to AFSOC missions is the U-28A, a single-engine plane used for *reconnaissance* and intelligence-gathering missions and which can also transport small groups of men. It is designed to fly in and out of crude runways made of grass or dirt. Just 47 feet (14 m) long with a wingspan of 53 feet (16 m), the plane has a range of 1,750 miles (2,800 km). It is especially useful for servicing remote locations in which a C-130 might not be practical.

To accomplish their missions, all STT personnel are heavily armed. The basic weapon is the Colt M4A1 carbine. A descendant of the M16 assault rifle, it has a shorter barrel that makes it better suited for close quarters combat. It typically includes the Rail Interface System (RIS), which allows the attachment of gunsights, laser lights, and even other armament onto the top, bottom, and both sides. Other weapons include the H&K MP5 submachine gun, Remington 870 12-gauge shotgun, M249 squad automatic weapon, Beretta M9 pistol, and M203 grenade launcher—the latter of which is either used by itself or attached to the underside of the M4A1.

That's just the start. All three types of STTs enter combat with their own sets of specialized gear. Pararescuemen need to treat everything from stubbed toes to severe trauma for up to 72 hours. They carry dozens of items, ranging from Band-Aids and Chapstick to materials for performing minor surgery. In some cases, they may even carry a smaller version of the Jaws of

*Handheld anemometers help special operations weathermen measure wind speed.*

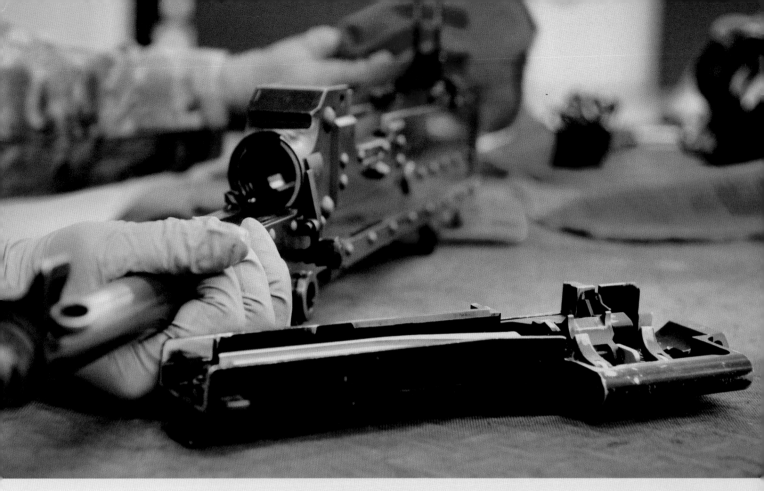

Life used by many civilian rescue workers.

Special operations weathermen need a variety of specialized instruments to perform their tasks. As Chris Carroll, a writer for the military newspaper *Stars and Stripes*, notes, "The missions are varied, and the specifics of most are classified, but a typical one involves slipping quietly into an area with Army Special Forces troops to lay the groundwork for a large operation. That could mean setting up networks of tiny, remote weather sensors, analyzing soil type and terrain so commanders can bring vehicles in or land aircraft, and gauging river depths and flow to make crossings safer." The operator may also inflate a balloon and send it aloft to get atmospheric readings.

Combat controllers carry what are perhaps the heaviest loads of all. The most vital piece of their equipment is the radio. As the authoritative Special Operations Forces Situation Report (SOFREP) points out, "Virtually anyone can fire a suppressed M4 or go loud with an M240B, but the guy talking in the B1s, B52s, and F15s on CAS runs has the most immediate bang at his disposal." One essential tool in generating that "bang" is a laser device used to

*Regular cleaning and inspection of weaponry and gear are essential in training and in the field.*

"paint" an enemy target. As one controller notes, "It's not some little handheld, pen-light thing. Those lasers weigh 60 pounds [27 kg]. That's in addition to the 60, 70 pounds of kit and weapons we're already carrying."

Another useful tool for a combat controller is the bat cam, a tiny, remote-controlled aircraft with a camera that weighs as little as two pounds (0.9 kg). In one instance, a combat controller was on patrol with an Army Special Forces unit, which was following the course of a riverbed. Suddenly, the bed took a sharp bend. "The combat controller pulled a bat cam out of his rucksack, started the engine, and launched it by hand to see what was ahead," explained Lieutenant General Woolsey. The device detected enemy positions, which were eliminated when the controller called in an air strike. The patrol was then able to continue without any American casualties.

Combat controllers also need to quickly sketch out a remote airfield. So they're likely to be packing equipment such as a survey set (to establish the boundaries of the field) and a clutch of tiny landing lights. Unsurprisingly, it's not unusual for the total weight of an operative's gear to exceed the weight of the man carrying it.

*The 352nd Special Operations Group uses three variants of MC-130 aircraft, including the Talon.*

**FORCE FACTS** In addition to conveying special forces personnel under any weather conditions, Hercules Combat Talons also dropped 15,000-pound (6,800 kg) "Daisy Cutter" bombs on targets in Afghanistan.

# MEMORABLE MISSIONS

AFTER THEIR SUCCESS IN DESTROYING THE RADAR INSTALLATIONS at the onset of Operation Desert Storm, AFSOC was called back into action four days later. A U.S. Navy F-14 Tomcat fighter had been shot down deep inside Iraqi-controlled territory. Though the pilot, Lieutenant Devon Jones, had ejected from the aircraft and landed in the desert, Iraqi forces were in hot pursuit. Capturing him would have been a major propaganda triumph for Saddam Hussein, who likely would have beamed the image of the prisoner around the world. Escorted by two "Warthogs"—A-10 Thunderbolt II ground-support fighter/bombers bristling with rockets and

machine guns—a pair of Pave Lows took off on a rescue mission. Unfortunately, the *coordinates* they had been given weren't accurate. After a lengthy search with no sign of the missing pilot, they had to return to base to refuel. Soon, they resumed the search. This time they were able to locate Jones by following his voice transmissions. However, the Iraqis were able to do the same thing. When the rescuers arrived at Jones's position, a truck full of Iraqi troops was moments away from capturing him. A blast from one of the Warthogs took out the truck. The Pave Lows set down, and Jones raced over to them. The helicopters immediately took off and whisked the lieutenant back to the safety of American lines.

After the 9/11 terrorist attacks on the World Trade Center, U.S. president George W. Bush wanted to retaliate. A team of U.S. Army Green Berets was inserted into Afghanistan in mid-October 2001. Accompanying them was Master Sergeant Bart Decker, an AFSOC

*Pave Low pilots earned more than 140 Silver Stars for valor in combat from 1967 to 2008.*

combat controller whose job was to call in air strikes against Taliban positions. As part of the mission, Decker and the other Americans had to ride horseback on wooden saddles—something they had never done before. In some ways, that mode of transportation seemed riskier than actual combat. "[The horses] were trying to scramble up the rocks, and their hooves, their shoes were sparking," Decker said. "You were worried about sliding off anytime, but you had to keep going.... We separated, especially at night, when we're walking on that ledge, because you put two horses together, all they wanted to do was fight. You look down at the left side, there's a 500-foot drop-off."

The men soon adjusted to their equine conveyors and began doing the job for which they were trained. Decker's role was crucial. He called in bombing coordinates to the navigator on an American aircraft hovering overhead. The navigator then relayed those coordinates to B-52 bombers flying six miles (9.6 km) above the targets. The navigator with whom Decker was communicating was a woman, and she was quickly nicknamed the "angel of death" by the Afghans who listened in on Decker's conversations with her. As he noted, "The warlord we were advising heard her on my radio and broadcast to the enemy: 'Female up in this airplane is wreaking havoc on you.' That's an insult, obviously, to the Taliban, who used to beat down their women."

Soon after the arrival of American special forces, a Taliban convoy of fuel trucks and other vehicles halted for the night near the Afghanistan–Pakistan border. The drivers fell asleep inside their cabs. Suddenly, they were yanked out, immobilized with plastic handcuffs, and taken a short distance away. Besides the men who were guarding them, other mysterious figures stood nearby, speaking softly into their radios. Soon, the prisoners heard the clatter of approaching helicopters. Moments later, fireballs soared hundreds of feet in the air as rockets ripped into the convoy. When the fires died down, the drivers were taken

*A container delivery system (CDS) drop is when supplies such as food and water are parachuted in.*

**FORCE FACTS** During Operation Anaconda, combat controllers called in air strikes against enemy combatants who were as close as 60 feet (20 m) from American positions.

back to the smoldering wreckage of their vehicles and released. They clambered onto a large, horse-drawn cart. "Have a safe trip," their attackers—one of several small units of combat controllers and pararescuemen—told them. "But spread the word." The word, along with the actions behind it, quickly spread.

Unfortunately, things didn't go as well the following March. Though the Taliban were no longer in overall control of Afghanistan, many of their fighters were still active in the country. One of their last major strongholds was in the mountainous province of Paktia, located in southeast Afghanistan along the border with Pakistan. Operation Anaconda, the first large-scale commitment of American conventional forces in the Afghan war, sought to drive them out. When the troops ran into stronger-than-expected resistance, American commanders wanted to establish an observation post on a high ridge overlooking the battlefield. Unfortunately, the Taliban had the same idea. A helicopter carrying Navy SEALs came under heavy fire. One man, Petty Officer Neil Roberts, fell from the aircraft. The helicopter crash-landed several miles away. A second helicopter, which included combat controller John Chapman, took off on a rescue mission. It, too, came under heavy fire, and Chapman was killed. Still another rescue helicopter took off, only to be shot down as well.

By now, a substantial group of wounded men had been assembled. It became the focal point for Taliban gunfire. Pararescueman Jason Cunningham, who was treating the wounded, was himself shot several times. He continued to administer first aid despite being in severe pain. He also moved the men under his care several times to try to keep them as safe as possible. With three helicopters already taken out, commanders didn't want to risk losing any more during daylight. By the time dusk had fallen and helicopters could operate in relative safety, Cunningham had died. For

*Captain Barry Crawford humbly expressed his gratitude upon receiving the Air Force Cross.*

his heroism and selfless devotion to the wounded, Cunningham was posthumously awarded the Air Force Cross. It is the nation's second-highest military decoration. While the operation on what was later named Roberts Ridge (in honor of Neil Roberts) killed more than 100 Taliban, 8 Americans—including Chapman and Cunningham—lost their lives. It was the largest loss of American lives in a single engagement in the war up to that point.

Eventually, the War in Afghanistan would become the longest in American history, and AFSOC personnel continued to play a vital role. In 2012, Captain Barry Crawford Jr. received the Air Force Cross for his actions during a firefight in Afghanistan two years earlier. A team of about 100 Green Berets and Afghan troops flew into a remote village to secure a suspected weapons *cache*. They came under intense sniper and machine-gun fire within a few minutes, and five Afghans were wounded. "Our placement in the middle of the village, and the enemy's superior fighting positions, required us to 'run the gauntlet' of enemy fire no matter where we were in the valley," Crawford said. Without regard for his own safety, Crawford—acting as a combat controller—ran into the open to

*In recent years, AFSOC operatives have put themselves in harm's way throughout Afghanistan.*

guide a medical evacuation helicopter. One incoming bullet shot away one of Crawford's radio antennas, just inches from his face. He also called in attacks against the enemy positions that eventually allowed the unit to move out of the ambush zone. Several hours later, the men encountered another ambush. With the enemy nearly as close as the length of a football field, Crawford again emerged in the open to direct aerial attacks that suppressed enemy fire. The entire engagement lasted for about 10 hours and resulted in the deaths of more than 80 enemy combatants. No Americans were killed, though unfortunately two of the wounded Afghans died. "Captain Crawford repeatedly and conspicuously disregarded his own safety to assist his United States and Afghan teammates," said air force Chief of Staff General Norton Schwartz. "It is not hard to be utterly impressed by his bravery and inspired by his selflessness."

Those same qualities could be used to describe the entire Air Force Special Operations Command. Members of AFSOC continue to be ready for action anytime, anywhere. Whenever support is needed, skilled AFSOC operatives are sure to answer the call.

*AFSOC weathermen provide support and gather information that can prove critical to a mission.*

**FORCE FACTS** During the War in Afghanistan, combat controllers were credited with 170 kills in close air support for every enemy combatant they shot with their carbines.

The Osprey's tilt-rotor design took several years to perfect; it entered service in 2009.

**FORCE FACTS** One advantage of the CV-22 Osprey is that it is much quieter than conventional helicopters, allowing it to achieve a high degree of surprise when it lands.

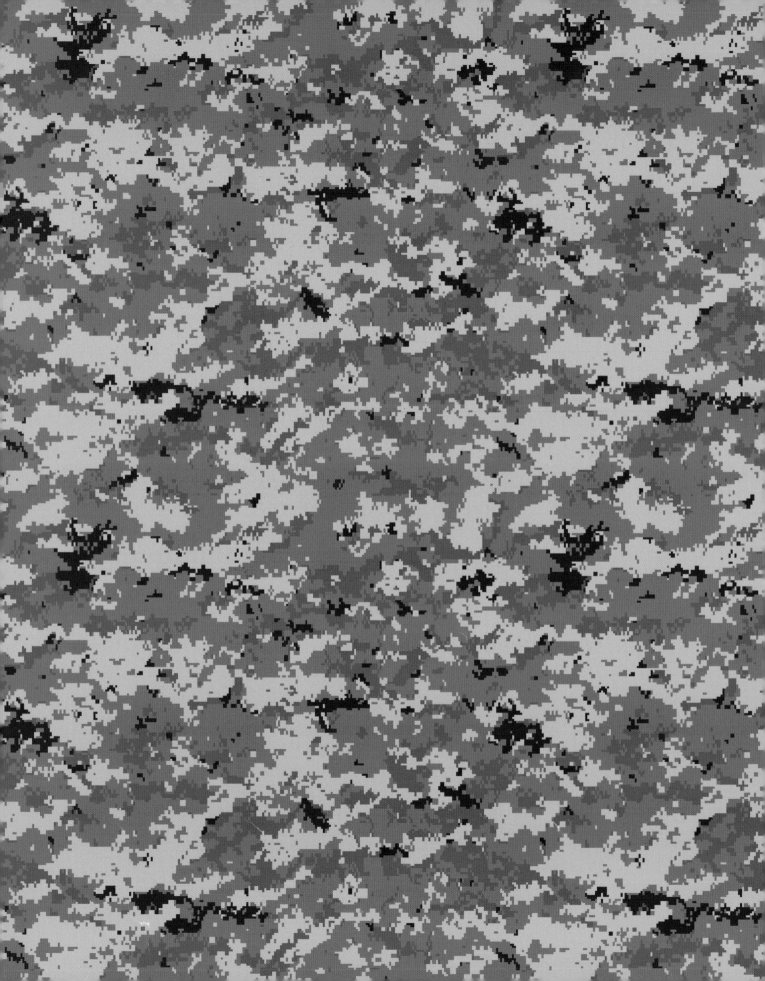

# GLOSSARY

*cache* – a concealed storage location

*casings* – the housings for bullets

*coordinates* – where the longitude and the latitude of a point on Earth intersect

*covert* – hidden, secret

*deployed* – moved personnel into position for military action

*fast-roping* – sliding down a thick rope suspended from a helicopter as rapidly as possible

*iconic* – something that is very famous and represents a particular thing or idea

*infrared* – a type of light that is invisible but indicates the presence of heat

*loadmaster* – an aircraft crew member who is in charge of loading and unloading its cargo

*nacelles* – streamlined housings on aircraft that cover and contain the engine and prop-rotor group

*propaganda* – information, especially biased or misleading, that is used to promote a cause or system of beliefs

*rappel* – descend a vertical surface using a rope coiled around the body and attached at a higher point

*reconnaissance* – a search to gain information, usually conducted in secret

*Taliban* – a fundamentalist Islamic political movement and militia that controlled Afghanistan; noted especially for terror tactics and a repressive attitude toward women

*theater of operations* – a large region in which military operations take place

**FORCE FACTS** Combat controllers are entitled to wear scarlet berets, which include a crest bearing the words "First there."

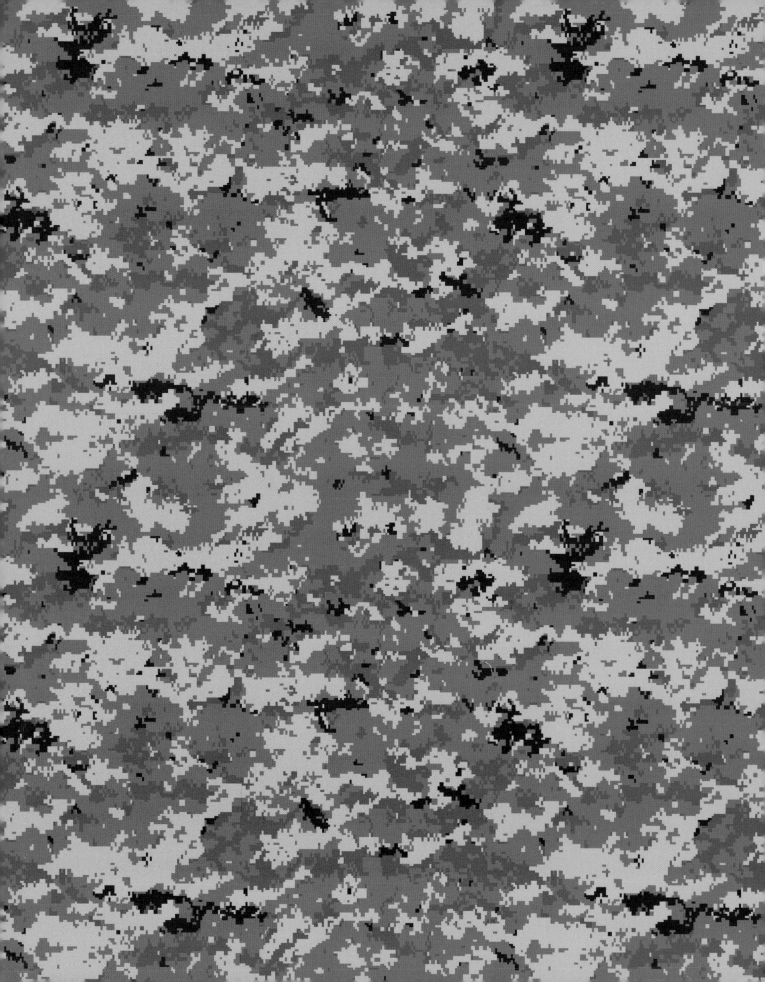

# SELECTED BIBLIOGRAPHY

U.S. SPECIAL FORCES

Cantrell, Mark, and David Vaughan. *Special Forces: America's Elite*. Bonita Springs, Fla.: The Media Source, 2012.

Carney, Col. John T., and Benjamin F. Schemmer. *No Room for Error: The Covert Operations of America's Special Tactics Units from Iran to Afghanistan*. New York: Ballantine Books, 2002.

North, Oliver. *American Heroes in Special Operations*. Nashville: Fidelis Books, 2010.

Pushies, Fred. *Deadly Blue: Battle Stories of the U.S. Air Force Special Operations Command*. New York: American Management Association, 2009.

————. *U.S. Air Force Special Ops*. St. Paul, Minn.: MBI Publishing, 2007.

Time-Life Books. *The New Face of War: Special Operations and Missions*. Alexandria, Va.: Time-Life Books, 1990.

Tucker, David, and Christopher J. Lamb. *United States Special Operations Forces*. New York: Columbia University Press, 2007.

Zimmerman, Dwight Jon, and John D. Gresham. *Beyond Hell and Back: How America's Special Operations Forces Became the World's Greatest Fighting Unit*. New York: St. Martin's Press, 2007.

# WEBSITES

**Air Force Special Operations Command**

*http://www.afsoc.af.mil/index.asp*

The official AFSOC website includes news, photos, history of AFSOC, information about enlistment and training, and more.

**Defense Media Network – AFSOC**

*http://www.defensemedianetwork.com/category /spec-ops/afsoc/*

This site offers in-depth articles and photos about various aspects of AFSOC, including summaries of activities by year.

# READ MORE

Brush, Jim. *Special Forces*. Mankato, Minn.: Sea-to-Sea, 2012.

Cooper, Jason. *U.S. Special Operations*. Vero Beach, Fla.: Rourke, 2004.

U.S. SPECIAL FORCES

# INDEX